Atoms and Building Blocks For Babies and Toddlers

Thabsile Thabethe & Luyanda Momodu

This is Lulu.

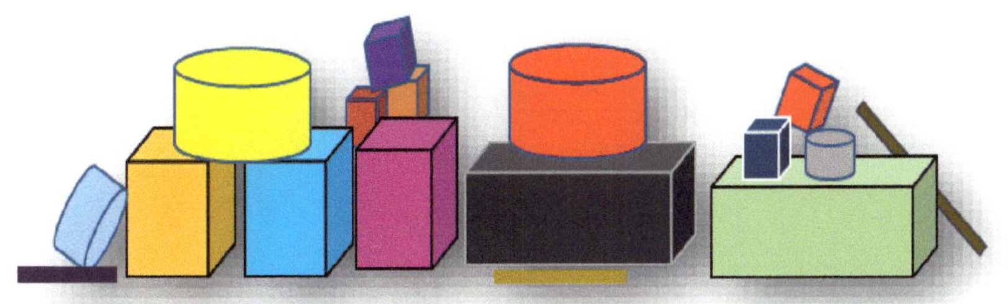

Lulu has building blocks.

She wants to make a

robot.

Can Lulu use one block

to make the robot?

No!

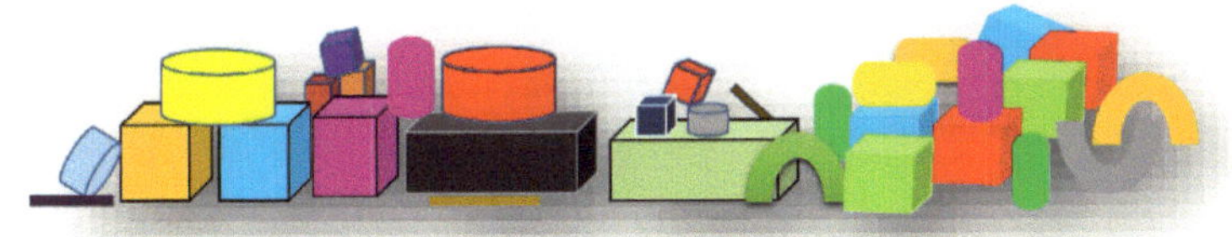

She needs many building blocks to make a robot.

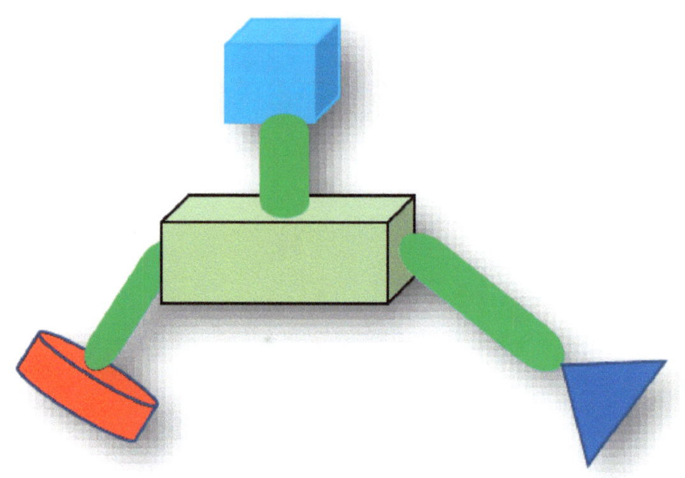

To build a robot, she has to combine the building blocks.

Lulu used different blocks with different colors to make the robot.

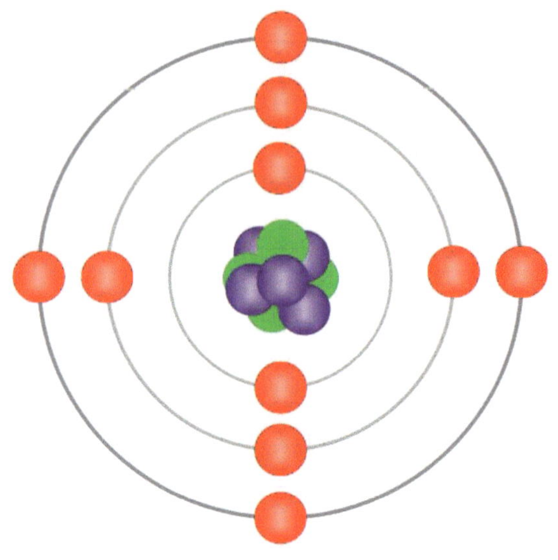

This is an atom.

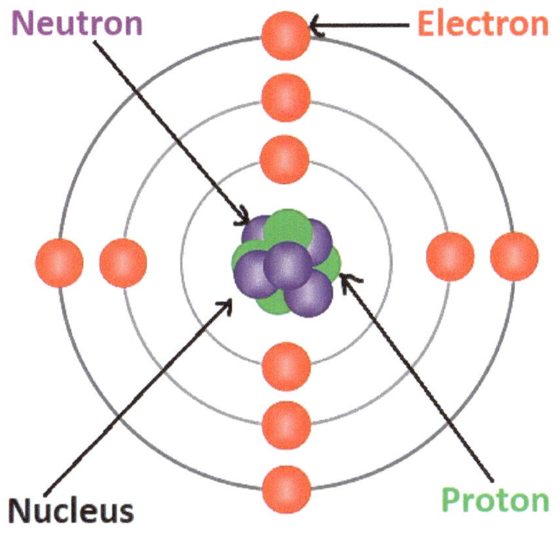

It has protons,

neutron and electrons.

The nucleus is at the

centre of the atom.

Atoms are tiny.

We cannot see them with our naked eyes.

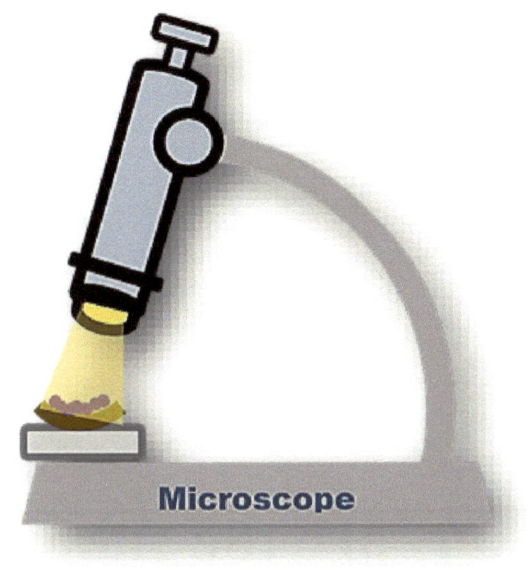

We need a microscope to see small objects.

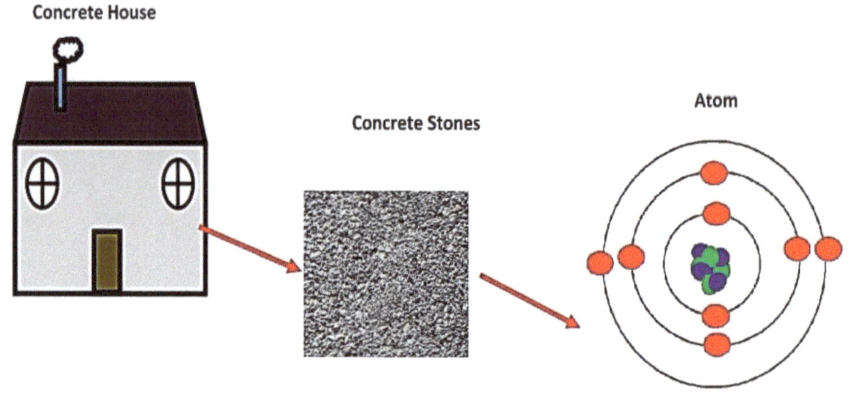

Atoms are the smallest building blocks.

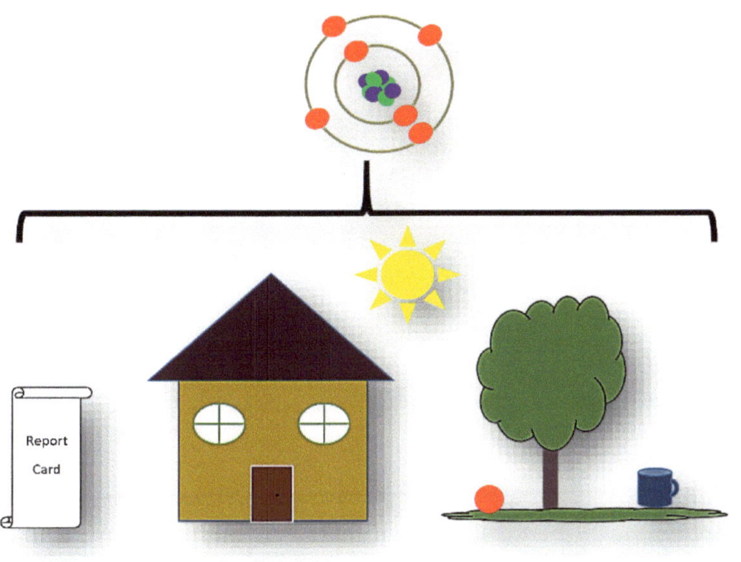

Everything is made up of atoms.

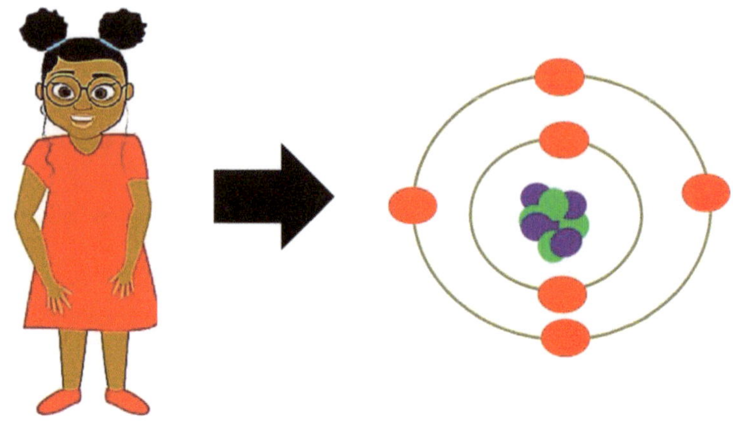

Humans are made up of atoms.

Many atoms combine to make a human.

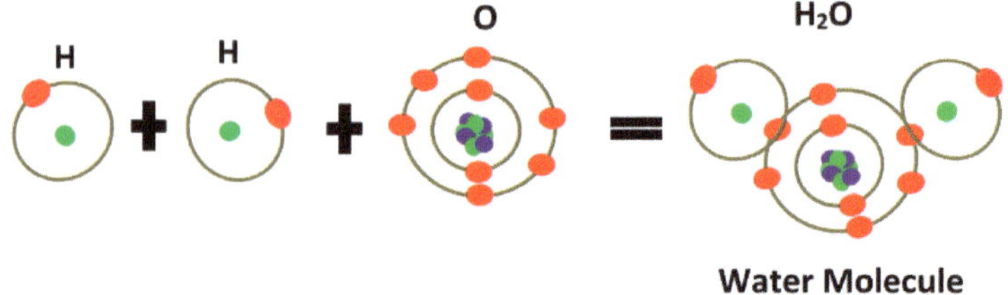

When atoms combine, they form a molecule.

Lulu used blocks of different colors, shapes and sizes to make the robot.

Different atoms are required to create human beings.

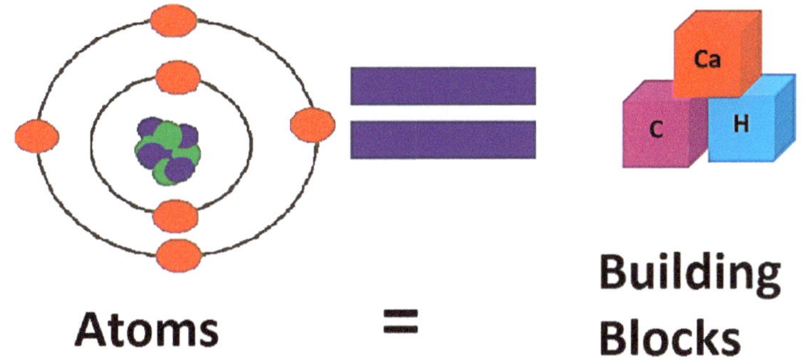

Atoms are buildings blocks.

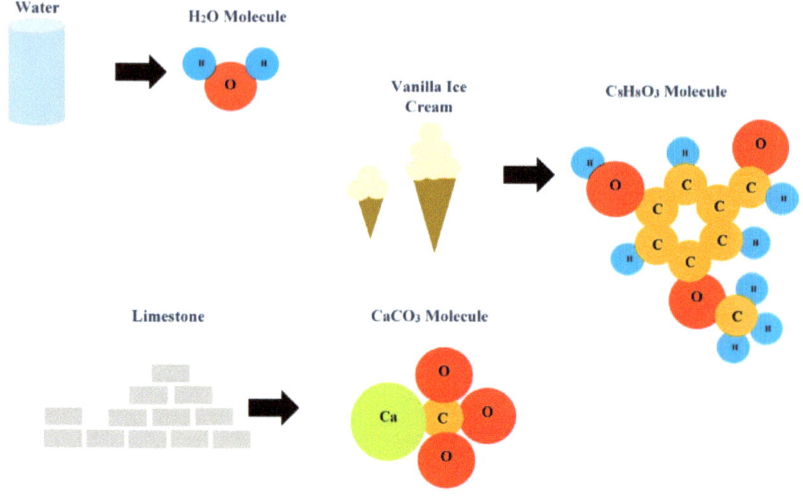

Because everything is made up of atoms.

Well done baby!

You have finished

reading your Atom

Book.

" The best time to learn is when you are still young and curious. "
Introduction to X-rays for Babies and Toddlers
Thermodynamics For Babies and Toddlers
Introduction to SUBTRACTION for Toddlers
Introduction to MATHEMATICS for Toddlers: Addition
Dr Thabsile Thabethe is a physicist, a researcher, a teacher and a mother. Luyanda Momodu is a 5 year old who loves reading, exploring (doing experiments) and playing.
Authors: Thabsile Thabethe and Luyanda Momodu
Text copyright 2022: Thabsile Thabethe and Luyanda Momodu
Illustration copyright: Thabsile Thabethe
Cover copyright: Lekeretla Modiadie
ISBN 978-0-620-98962-6
9 780620 989626
90000>

•

www.ingramcontent.com/pod-product-compliance
Lightning Source LLC
LaVergne TN
LVHW021325160826
845679LV00001B/470

* 9 7 9 8 8 3 1 4 1 9 1 0 8 *